Ratko Delorko's Piano Police

Declutter Your Playing With Snackable Nuggets of Pianistic Wisdom

AF177591

A 40-Page Guide to Better Playing. In a Half-Hour Read.

After many failed attempts and setbacks, today I can share with you the experience and insights I have gained over the years and certainly show you some shortcuts or put you on the fast track. This is also called pragmatic learning and conveys a high problem-solving potential. I created the idea of the Piano Police to give you simple, actionable, bite-sized strategies to help you declutter your playing and feed you with snackable nuggets of pianistic wisdom. If you're an ambitious teacher or performer, or one in the making or on the rise, who is really looking to create a pianistic approach that makes an impact and music you love, you're in the best place. Let's dive in.

ZK 5277

Imprint

Softcover: ISBN 978-3-384-31760-5

E-Book: ISBN

Text, Pics & Cover: © 2024 Copyright by
                        Ratko Delorko
Editor: English Translation
                        David Andruss
Technical terms: Darin Niebuhr
Content: Ratko Delorko Zeitklang
                        Eichendorffstr. 31
                        45219 Essen
                        zeitklangmedia@gmx.de
                        www.delorko.com
Print & Distribution: tredition GmbH,
                        Ahrensburg, Germany

Index

First a Little Trivia:

Hey there! Greetings from my little slice of the Piano Business. I'm Ratko Delorko, pianist, composer, producer, educator and author. I've got a side hustle at the Piano Police as a Piano Police Officer. At the moment, there's an incoming emergency call at the Piano Police Operations Center from a desperate pianist. I offer some advice on how to cope with the situation. Happy reading. Over and out.

How to buy a Piano

Ringelingeling. A very nervous pianist calls.

You've reached the Piano Police. What's the nature of your emergency?

The guy is totally in panic mode. Blablablabulb. Difficult to understand...

You want to buy a piano? A used one? Shall we send a piano investigation team? No? Then first check the outer appearance: A clean and well-maintained instrument already gives an indication of its inner state of care. Wreaths of flower vases under crocheted doilies are silent witnesses of misunderstood home decor. Many a droplet of brackish water will have found its way into the innermost part over the years. Also look out for peeling, wavy veneer and chipped or cracked pieces of polyester. The glossy black varnish happily chips at the corners. These are sure signs of brusque jostling or heavy moisture contact and thus expected expensive repairs. The paint should not have deep scratches, chipping or pressure marks. Repairs are expensive and usually unsatisfactory. There may well be unavoidable signs of use such as fine scratches from dusting without furniture spray or chamber music partners depositing their cases on the big shiny surface.

Telltale spots where light dust accumulates indicate an active woodworm. In this regard, a look under the grand into the beams is also worthwhile. Occasionally these little animals are quite aggressive and turn a supposedly inexpensive barn find into a disaster. Old, uninhabited holes are harmless, however.

The question arises: How to spot a Worn Piano?

What do the pedals look like? They are hosted in the lyre. Do they have any side clearance? If the right pedal is heavily worn compared to the left one, and the key covering in the middle of the keyboard is considerably worn, too, this already indicates plenty of playing hours.

Keyboard: The keyboard covering, if it is still made of ebony & ivory, please check for legal issues. The covers must be complete and undamaged. No plates are glued with „Elmer's glue-all“. You can detect this by the yellowish dirt oozing out of one edge. General yellow discoloration is a blemish that can be fixed quite easily. How to do it? No - hands off. Your piano tech does it with hydrogen peroxide and sun or UV light. Just like a hairdresser. The keys should have hardly any lateral clearance and should not jam under lateral pressure. Keys that are audibly rubbing against each other are crying out for a new garnish: The cashmere cloth that guides the keys must be replaced. Hard work. Are the lead weights, which can be seen on the side when the adjacent key is pressed, oxidized and blossomed? Then sudden key jams are imminent.

Open sesame: The first look under the lid is for all the pretty colored felt ribbons that are placed under strings or artfully woven in. If there is moth damage, the hammer heads and damper pads will also have been on the menu of these cute flying creatures. If the piano is not grandma's family heirloom, I would close the lid now and leave. Dust is not bad, but a thick coating tells stories about the general state of care. Sticky stains on the soundboard and on action parts indicate that flower vases or drinks have been tipped over. Severe consequences may appear.

```
*****************************************************
```

Nugget: Sometimes, playing piano is lighthearted and fun. It's not always super serious or super introspective or something philosophical.

```
*****************************************************
```

The guy seems to be on a tiny budget and is afraid of expensive repair jobs. What to consider?

On a grand piano: Do all dampers appear to be absolutely parallel? Are there obvious flaws on the copper of the bass strings? Are strings missing? Are the steel strings bright steel or black and rust stained? Or nicotine-stained? Rusty strings are not sonic gems, but they are a sure indicator of excessive humidity. Thick nicotine coating produces a noticeable loss of treble and overtones in the sound - you wouldn't believe it. Does the soundboard have cracks? These are very easy to spot, as are cracks in the bridge in the area of the bridge pins. These are the spots where the majority of buzzes come from inside a piano. So-called "wind cracks" are only superficial and not critical. However, this is better judged later by the piano tech.

Does the soundboard show bulges? Does its varnish look cracked? Are all the tuning pins in line? Do they tilt their heads forward under the string load and their hole has become an oval? Does the pin block (wrest plank), which is sometimes not covered by the cast iron plate, have cracks? All of these things are repairable, but sometimes with considerable effort, so that the supposedly inexpensive offer is basically an economic total loss. A look at the hopefully available serial number on the frame and other matching parts like the fall board, music rack, keyslip, the action frame or on the cheek or side blocks, can't hurt. In connection with the corresponding manual, the year of manufacture can be determined.

The inner values: Today, there are close to 1,400 moving parts made of wood, metal and cashmere working behind the scenes for your dynamic piano playing. That's why an upright or grand piano is soooo expensive to buy. Alone the technical apparatus makes up a huge chunk. Reason enough to take a closer look and bring the action to light. Have you ever tried it on your own instrument? Make sure that all hammers are in rest position before you pull out the action (grand piano). Do not even think about pressing any key while pulling out the action. You will be punished immediately with a harsh noise telling you that you cracked a few hammer shanks and the repair will cost a lot of money. Hope you dig that. Then we'll do that right away. But before that, it makes sense to learn something about the complex processes behind the fall board.

Whether it's an upright or a grand piano, the key itself is a mere lever. Nothing more. It is guided by two blank pins and its dip is 10 mm. At its end sits a thick, polished brass screw, the so-called capstan. Its job is to put your momentum into the complex action. Up to this point, the piano and the grand piano are the same.

Grand piano: A triangle that moves in itself, called wippen, is pushed upwards by the key via the capstan and accelerates a shank attached to an axle, with the hammer at its end, against the string. Beneath the shank sits a small leather-covered roller called hammer knuckle, almost the thickness of your pinky. It rests on the upper part of the triangle (called the repetition lever) and awaits its thrust. Then, when it goes up, at the last moment the front (player-facing) part of the triangle (named the jack) tilts forward and gives the knuckle the final kick (called let-off) when the jack-toe hits the let-off button and the hammer is airborne towards the string.

****
Nugget: Failure is success in progress.

****

Has the Hammer to be Treated? *The guy is totally clueless...*

The hammer—btw. a worn hammer can be resurfaced down maybe twice in its life—having traveled a path of 47 mm upward against gravity, has successfully bounced against the string, causing it to vibrate with its focussed energy. The energy is conducted via the bridge into the soundboard, where it first becomes audible to us. Because the string only, no matter how wildly it vibrates, is not capable of setting sufficient air molecules in motion. For this, the soundboard is the appropriate medium.

At the halfway point of the hammerhead's travel, the end of the key has moved the damper resting on the string upward via a lever and a wire, releasing the string. This moment is called the halfway point. Clear the way for the tone to follow in a moment. Once bounced off the string, the hammer plops its back in the middle of its return path into the back check, which stands rigidly on a fixed wire at the end of the key. It is a quite resilient and small wooden block covered with felt and leather.

Under the upper part of our wippen, the repetition lever, sits a coil for which it became tense: The repetition lever was pushed down a bit in its center pin by the fallen-back hammer resting in the back check and its shank and knuckle. As a result, it compresses the spring, which, in the event of any repetition and the associated early release of the key, opens the lever link a bit and brings the jack back into the position ready to move the knuckle again. The whole thing is called "double action" developed by Erard in the 1820s. The point of all this: The key does not have to return to its rest position to be ready for action again, as was the case with the old fortepianos and harpsichords, but can be reactivated at 2/3 of its travel. This simplifies and speeds up the repetition and also allows for a rather slow legato repetition.

Really? He wants to learn how the hammer is constructed...

Many superimposed (wool) piles are rolled into a felt sheet. Then it is cut, shaped, and pressed over the wedge-shaped core to form a huge hammerhead blank, which is then sawn into the appropriate hammerheads. These are then stripped (sanded) and voiced (stabbed) with needles by the piano tech after being glued onto the shanks and installed into the action. This process of voicing specifically affects the tension in the felt to produce a more brilliant or softer tone color.

The ratio of the key's 10mm depth to the hammerhead's 47mm travel creates a 1:4.7 gain. So everything you feed to the key arrives at the string almost 5 times as strong. To make sure that these ratios are correct, your instrument must not only be tuned from time to time, but also voiced and regulated properly. After all, you take your car in for a check and don't just drive it through the car wash after fueling it up. More about this at the end.

Basically, the structure described is the same as that of the upright piano. The only difference is that the hammer head of the upright piano does not have to be guided against gravity. Nor does it assist in its fall back. A thin ribbon (bridle strap) is supposed to help with this, but in an emergency it is simply overtaxed. Except for a small curve, the hammer head hits the string almost horizontally. Precisely for these reasons, the piano is inferior to a grand piano in its playing possibilities. There is also no lifting wippen in this sense, but rather a hammer knuckle over a rather long striking jack and a catcher, which is supposed to be grabbed by the back check. This works most of the time, but the controlled feel-good experience of a good grand action doesn't want to surface.

Enough of the basics, now the action must be brought to light.

Do I really have to pull the action out? *Every player should be capable of this!*

On the grand piano: Remove the fall board by pulling it upwards out of its guides. Occasionally, it is additionally secured against mischief by small screws—mostly un-necessary—which like to disappear, never to be seen in any crevices. Or the screws fall out if you have been too generous with the turns and can then hardly be screwed back in again within a quarter of an hour. It is and re-mains a miserable fiddling....

Steinways have had the same unfortunate system for more than 140 years: After you have removed the screws from the cheek blocks, you carefully remove the stubborn attachment bar (keyslip) in front of the keyboard, which tends to suddenly give way and jump loose, tearing off an ivory key top in the process perhaps. Then lift the fall board together with the cheek blocks out as straight as possible. If the lid is not straight in the process, the cheek blocks will fall out of their holder and rumble to the floor. If there is a carpet, you are lucky. If the cheek blocks fall onto a stone floor, the high glossy surface will be dam-aged. Annoying and expensive. Installation is just as im-practical.

With other brands: You have happily lifted out the fall board. You have also successfully loosened and removed the screws from the cheek blocks on the right and left un-der the console, and then take out the cheek blocks. These will usually then reveal the easy-to-remove keyslip in front of the keyframe. While you are at it, take a look at any moth infestation of the under felts of the keys. Check the visible key pins for corrosion by using a flashlight.

You can grab the action either by the frame or by the two metal pins on the left and right of the keyboard frame. Before doing this, look through the strings from above to make sure that all the hammer heads are in their resting position. That's where they should stay... I rock the action back and forth a bit at the beginning to avoid sudden resistance. You may also call me paranoid. Then pull the action forward, s l o w l y and mega cautiously, never touching a key, until you can reach under the keyboard frame to carefully pull the action further forward and then lift it out by the frame. Anyone who thinks my precautions regarding the hammer heads are exaggerated will be punished with a loud "Hrrrtsch". This is how a hammer head that has just broken off presents itself to us acoustically; usually it doesn't stay with just one. The following call to the piano technician is first embarrassing, then expensive. Just as meticulously, the action is put back into place. Every now and then, internal but clearly visible components of the pedals get in the way. With a little pedal movement, you will master that...

****

Nugget: If you go the independent route, you'll hit roadblocks. If you go independent you need a certain level of resilience, and you need to be ready to invest both money and time in yourself.

****

On the upright: The upper frame, that's the lid you always stare at, wants to be removed. Before you do that, you have to close the fall board! On the top right and left sit small locking devices that first want to be unlocked. You remove the bulky but light part by tilting it a bit towards you and then lifting it out. Now the key cover may be opened again and if you're lucky, it doesn't interfere with the action. Otherwise, you'll also have to lift it upwards out of its fiddly guides without canting it, perhaps it needs to be unscrewed. Otherwise, it will jam stupidly. Now loosen the shiny brass screws that keep the action in place. Then tilt the action a little towards you and you can take them out upwards. It's not always so easy with upper dampers, since the dampers sit above the action. In principle, upper dampers that do not dampen very well can be converted to modern lower damping in the course of a restoration. However, this is not cheap and not always worthwhile. I think, by the way, the upper dampers do not lack a certain charm.

You are unsure about all the technology? Then you better hire a piano tech to help you on the spot. But actually you can do this....

Where to look first?

The first look is at the hammer heads. How bad are the signs? If you lightly scratch over them with your finger-nail and noticeably catch, the head needs to be resurfaced and filed. Your piano technician will do this by filing the head until the signs are gone. He must decide whether there is enough material left for this - replacements are expensive. If the felt is very dirty, it looks shabby, but probably it has not been resurfaced at all or rarely and its substance is good. Small craters on the flanks indicate moth damage. By the way, moths don't seem to like Asian felts. Why this is so, I do not know.

Very lightly swipe once across the row of hammer heads. Does one wobble more than the others? Then the center pin will be knocked out. On the grand, lift the heads and drop them. The fall back must be prompt. If the heads fall back tenaciously, the axles are much too tight due to cor-rosion. The piano tech refers to this as "tight center pins."

If you want to be absolutely sure, unscrew some hammer flanges from the main action rail for testing purposes. Then take the end that was screwed onto the action rail between your thumb and forefinger. Bravely swing the hammer head back and forth and then let it swing. It must swing back and forth freely at least four times and then stop softly. If it stays jerky or tough, take note: The axles probably need to be changed. If it swings freely, perhaps even in very small movements, but not more than 8 times back and forth everything is fine. When you screw the flange back in, make sure it is parallel to its counterparts and turn its screw a half turn to the left first, very sensitive people will then feel a soft "plop" under the screwdriver so that the original thread will grab again when you turn the screw back in clockwise. Otherwise you will cut a new thread and the wood of the action rail or the tube will surely resent this.

What tube? *Pure curiosity...*

For ages, Steinways have had brass tubes (hammer rails) on which the hammer flanges are mounted. Implanted in the brass tube is a round wooden bar, sort of like a giant dowel for the screws. The system is not inexpensive to manufacture, but the feel is just fine. Replacement is expensive. The common wooden action bar is simpler and cheaper, some companies also use aluminum bars.

What to consider on an upright? *The guy seems to fire up...*

For the upright: Are all the bridle straps still attached? For the more technically minded: Compare the contact points of the hammer knuckle and the jack. Is the wear similar on all of them?

On a grand piano: Are the knuckles under the hammer shank still round, or are they flat at the contact points?

Before recommending a purchase, coordinate all repairs, regulation and voicing job (the pricking of the felt with a needle) with your piano repair shop.

Well in tune: A freshly tuned piano always gives a good impression. Nevertheless, you should check the pitch with your 440 tuning fork. Oh, you don't have one? Get an electronic tuning app for your phone. If the instrument is clearly below 440, your tuner will have to decide whether the instrument can be "pitch raised"; after all, you don't want to play a historical tuning with 426 or 432 Hz if you want to play along with other instruments. But: On my private 1898 upright I play 432. The instrument behaves well, sounds pretty and my ear feels less stress. No problem at all, because in my living room I don't play chamber music. Too much is unhealthy: There are instrument owners who torture their pianos up to 448 Hz. for whatever reason. This has nothing to do with modern sound sensibility, but only stresses all components and the hearing unnecessarily. It feels unhealthy for me.

He wants to find out...

For experienced people: Please ask the piano owner in advance if you are allowed to use the tuning hammer.

Check one tuning pin in each pin block region as a sample by carefully turning it counterclockwise, i.e. lower, while striking the note. If you feel that you have to help it to move minimally, it looks healthy. If it "slips away" immediately, caution is called for; the piano tech can measure the torque and will tell you more. Especially the last bass pins tend to be critical. Attention, possible string breakage is on your bill when bringing them back into tune. Ask the owner or dealer if a set of repair pins has already been installed in the course of a previous overhaul. They are a little bit thicker than the original pins. One oversize is fine, from the second oversize on, tunability and sound suffer and eventually a new pinblock is due. This is expensive fun. The piano tech will use calipers to determine the exact size of the pins. He may also have a torque gauge for the pin grip that will give accurate information about the real pin grip in both directions. If you discover pins in different sizes in different regions of the pin block - hands off, that was an inexpensive quick fix. Dark smudges around the pins indicate the forbidden use of pin-time pin block spray. The slight odor of WD 40 also indicates misuse.

What about the climate conditions?

Ideal climate: The climatic conditions of the location determine the life span of a keyboard instrument. Ideal is 48% relative humidity at 20 degrees Celsius. A tolerance of 10% is fine; above that, the corrosion and oxidation processes kick in more intensively, all felt parts swell and the wood soaks up delicate moisture. If the humidity is below the target, there is a risk of cracks in wooden parts. Severe fluctuations in humidity stress the instrument and eventually cause warping, poor tuning and cracking. If the piano of your choice is located on a cold exterior wall, condensation will certainly be found from behind it. In summer, the sun will then slam through the window on the south side and barbecue the black varnish, and in winter the underfloor heating will do the bad job. Instruments positioned in this way are ticking time bombs. Furthermore, finds from cellars and barns are exposed to moisture. At the location you are happy about the still fantastic pin grip, after the first heating period in the house of the new owner comes then the disillusionment, when the tuner shows up. The now finally thoroughly dried wrest plank (pinblock) gives free rein to its pins ...

****

Nugget: Work in Silence, Celebrate in Private - People love to ruin Things.

****

...but I have an expensive underfloor heating.
The guy is close to tears.

The best manufacturers and the most expensive uprights and grand pianos are powerless against misalignments and underfloor heating. The cozy underfloor heating extracts all the necessary residual moisture in the various woods from the instrument in the most effective way. Result: Cracks after a few years in elementary important parts like soundboard and possibly pinblock. The pins become loose and parts with previously exact fits rattle. This does not correspond to normal aging, because the instrument was not kept "species-appropriate".

The guy is howling...

The only remedy is to rip out the underfloor heating. Or don't use it consequently. I'd do that and risk the family squabble. Or: The installation of a Dampp-Chaser system. This is an evaporator that makes the instrument "all-around happy" and is very effective if you don't forget to refill it and don't spill either.

Generally, in winter, the room will need to be humidified, which is also good for your bronchial tubes; Don't forget to change filters... in summer, it will probably need to be dehumidified. These devices are now available inexpensively at hardware stores. The hygrometer decides what to do. It is a life-saving measure for the instrument. It will thank you for this effort with minor fluctuations in tone quality (an instrument that is too damp will sound dull), better tuning, longer maintenance intervals and intact woods. Here's to a long life!

And what about the tone?

The tonal test is probably the most subjective program item of all. To start with: Ignore possible harshness in the sound. It can be well corrected by the voicing of the hammer. Much more important is what you hear behind it. Pay attention to the tone length (sustain) in the range from C2 to C3. This melody position causes massive problems for all brands, old and young. Tone lengths of four seconds or longer without a noticeable bend in volume are good. Listen to single notes in the instrument to see how the overtone series develops. Octave, fifth and tenth should be discernible. Pay attention to whether triads held long in the middle register – try different triads in intervals of thirds and listen if they resonate and reflect at various points on the back of the rim and the lid. This brings color into play and a nice panorama of sound in the room. Or the triads are positioned on one side of the soundboard and seem to come from the hammer line. This sounds rather neutral and matter-of-fact, perhaps colorless.

Strike the basses where the strings are wound with copper pretty hard. Rattling bass strings that bring a soft "bzzz" along with the desired frequency need to be replaced. A high-frequency clack when struck will expose a loose hammer. Is there anything else that rattles? Noises that cannot be located can at best point to a loose lid hinge, at worst to a loose soundboard rib; a case for the piano technician. How is the feel? Tough or too directly responsive? Subjectively not the same? Does it audibly „rch–rch" when you press several keys at once very slowly? Then it's time for a regulation and the elimination of frictional resistance.

More testing

Try to create an even, widely distributed crescendo on single notes from ppp to fff. If this is only possible to a limited extent, or if the forte range enters suddenly, at least voice the hammers. With the right pedal depressed, make a glissando across all keys or perform a fat arm cluster. Then slowly release the pedal (incremental release) and listen to whether the damping does its job evenly. Do the dampers whistle then perhaps? If noticeably longer runaways remain when incrementally raising the pedal and bringing the dampers back onto the strings, then fiddly adjustment work is required here as well. If the treble dampens a little later than the bass, this may be wrong from a piano-tech point of view, but musically it is fine, because the melody treble can then shine with many overtones when the pedal is used with sensitivity.

The agony of choice: The second-hand market is huge. Small pianos, as they were modern in the 60s, are acoustically and mechanically unsatisfactory. From a height of 1.20 m onwards, I consider a piano to be a serious instrument that promises musical results. Feel good at the piano. Grand pianos under 1.80 m in length should not come into your choice, because the acoustic properties are not sufficient even with noble brands and can sometimes be worse than with an upright piano, due to major inharmonicities.

Inharmonywhat?

Inharmonicities are interfering, unwanted overtones such as the fourth, seventh and ninth. The simple test to do at home: Please play a C major triad starting with the key C. Sounds great. One octave lower is still ok. Two octaves lower, the triad begins to rattle audibly. On the early fortepianos, this phenomenon is much less audible due to the thinner strings. Finally, if you play the triad in the last lower octave, you will hear - nothing, just an undefined, dark concoction of sound. Completely useless, because the common upright or grand piano has to operate with very thick copper-wound strings due to its reduced height or length. Why? In order to reproduce the low frequencies, the string needs a defined, fairly high mass in relation to its tension, which is generated by a thick copper winding. It is actually a physical virtual length. This is one of the reasons why a concert grand is longer than the domestic baby grand and has less inharmonicity than its little brother, i.e. the tonal images in the low mid-range are clearly purer.

Buying an instrument in a well-run specialist store is a safe bet, because no reputable dealer is in the mood for endless complaints. There you make yourself known as a piano teacher. The dealer will then try very hard to advise your protégé well, you should come back and he would like to do the service later. Often there is a small commission for your good advice. Distrust garage dealers who don't know you and who bang their hand on the fresh, blue-black shiny piano lid and claim with conviction that the old instrument for the small price has been completely restored and is better than new. Used car dealers corresponding to this status also fill banana peels into the rear axle and sawdust into the transmission. Regardless of the company, high-quality work has its price. Such garage instruments have often been restored under catastrophic conditions in eastern climes. Remember: Good work ain't cheap and cheap work ain't good, but potentially expensive later.

My tip: Resist tempting commission offers. Rather pass on your potential price advantage. Your student will thank you through loyalty and the piano dealer will recognize that you recommend an instrument out of your professional understanding and not because the commission beckons. You won't get rich with the usual 5% anyway, but it is a kind gesture that may strengthen the hopefully long-lasting teaching relationship. This is also called customer loyalty. Thus you remain independent and the dealer knows that you can also go to the neighbor. Maybe he'll give you a freebie as a token of his appreciation and everyone will be happy. Win win. Talk to him openly about your wishes and sound ideas. A reputable company will always try to satisfy you as a professional within the possible range of the offer. Stay away from price negotiations. If your customer only wants it to come cheap and tries to figuratively twist the dealer's arm behind his back, it doesn't reflect well on you.

How to find a budget piano?

Attractive bargains like "Piano, new, € 1.500,- with bench, transport and tuning" are not serious. It literally carries the stench of fraud. Behind such offers hides not playable and not to be made playable keyboard furniture with German-sounding fantasy names in wrong spellings. With the right amount of moisture, green branches are likely to sprout from the boxes. This is trash from some

Far Eastern container at the price per kilo, whose environmentally friendly disposal also costs money.

All brands that start with "Stein..." or end with "...er" have a good reputation and are therefore often overpriced on the second-hand market. They create in the heads of the owners the thought to be able to make money with it even in scrap condition and therefore call up fantasy prices. Let others indulge in the exaggerated brand awareness and acquire these instruments. Pay attention to the inner values and you will not need to pay for a lesson.

Could it be something new after all? German manufacturers are basically more stable in value than the Japanese manufacturers. Qualitatively, the Japanese alternatives are absolutely equal, if one does not go straight to the cheap line. When it comes to reselling a German brand, you will get back almost all the money you once invested. In the case of Japanese instruments, as with cars, the rate of decay is much higher. Korean manufacturers are even more extreme, and Chinese products eventually may generate disposal costs.

Better buy from a private source or see a dealer?

New or used - I always buy from a piano dealer I trust. On the one hand, he offers a considerable selection, also from different manufacturers; on the other hand, the instruments of the higher categories are selected and technically prepared for sale, often with much effort and love. He will also let you try the instruments of your choice with angelic patience and give you conscientious advice. It is a decision for a long time, possibly over generations, so test who binds forever.

Of course, there can be Ebay bargains - but the probability is vanishingly small; therefore, it is all the more likely that the supposed bargain will end up being expensive fun. In contrast, the specialist dealer always has a reputation to lose and will be meticulous in every transaction to ensure that he does not receive any complaints, because these in turn cause costs and butcher his profit, which is not immense anyway. He must also be responsible for the used instruments and will be careful not to foist a cucumber on you. He must grant a two-year warranty on used instruments and possibly also provide a real warranty. That is what the word means. The garage dealer should not care, because after some time his garage is somewhere else....

What about restored or reconditioned pianos?

In the East, mainly in Poland, there are companies that specialize in restoring uprights and grand pianos and re-export them to the West. As always, there are these and those. A few of them meet the highest standards and even bring pianos back to life that should actually be disposed of – according to the principle: Better than new. Impressive, really impressive. Others, however, botch things up expertly. Especially after the fall of the iron curtain, there was a lot of bungling. Buyers who were delighted at the time are now selling these boxes. There are also "stein..." or "...er" instruments to be found. Superficially, you can recognize such instruments by the not deep black, but bluish shiny glossy surface (polyesther) and the hitch pins painted in gold bronze (to which the string is attached to the cast-iron frame), which should actually be steel colors.

What's the best piano?

The best piano on the market is the one that is fully paid for. You don't want to sit at your beloved instrument and think about the next payment. Leasing is for professionals who can make each payment tax deductible. This is not always without danger: If a payment "pops", i.e. you cannot service the leasing payment for whatever reason, your credit rating is shot. An installment plan can be an option for beginners; if you don't want to continue to play the piano, you can simply return the instrument. If you want to keep it, the rent will be offset against the normally higher purchase price.

Which brands do you recommend?

Me? Sorry. That's not on my payroll. Above a certain cat-
egory, all are in the "good" range, so this is private and
very personal. And preferences, as we all know, are 1000s
of thousands.... You might as well ask me if I prefer
blonde, brunette, black haired or red haired ladies. I
would be completely overwhelmed with the answer, be-
sides I am married.

Those who appreciate crisp and brilliant tone will find
themselves playing instruments with "duplex scales" (an
area in the string ends that resonates at desired frequencies, adding acoustic spice to the tone) and the capo d'as-
tro bar (string deflection at the cast-iron frame in the treble).

I prefer soft sounding instruments...

If you feel comfortable with a more romantic sound, you
will look for an instrument with a pressure bar (has the
same function as the capo, but it is screwed) or even with

continuous agraffes (have the task of keeping the string, which is under high tension, in the correct plane), and may also find it in an older instrument.

**Does a famous brand also require mainte-
nance? Or is it sufficient to get a tuning job
done from time to time?** *Jeez, he is such a
smart buyer...*

Shall we send a maintenance patrol car? No? A modern keyboard instrument is quite undemanding. It does, however, expect at least semi-annual tuning intervals—much more in professional use—and a 1.5-year technical check-up for moderate playing use. This includes light shaving of the hammer heads (the string marks are ground out of the felt and its original shape is preserved), their voicing (too hard and too soft consistencies and the associated timbres are compensated for by moderate stinging), and a balancing regulation of the entire action. This delays wear and tear, and the reward is always a pleasant playing experience and a beautiful tone.

Without these service intervals, the most famous instrument brands in the world cannot win a flower pot. Even if you drive a luxury automobile, but save on oil changes and brake jobs, you will find after a year and a day that only refueling and washing are not enough, and nights on the rain-soaked highway will bring long waits for roadside assistance. With the following bill, the garage can't stop laughing. It makes sense—doesn't it?

How to select an instrument? *We are getting serious...*

I would now like to give you some selection criteria that have proven themselves. This works regardless of brand and on both upright and grand pianos. Once three favorite instruments have emerged, you can start playing and be fairly certain that your hearing will not tire. Of course, at the end it is a musical decision—according to one's own listening and playing preferences. What must not happen under any circumstances is that, after a long selection, you end up with an instrument at home that you are not really satisfied with. It is crucial not to let yourself be influenced by trusting selection criteria such as: "Oh, that one sounds so hard," or, "Ah, but it's soft". These are all variables that can be changed afterwards by expert voicing. The important thing is that the potential is good, everything else can be adjusted.

In addition, there is the tactile feeling. How does the key surface feel? Does it promise to be a slippery ride on acrylic, or does the yellowish stuff feel sticky? You can't change anything about the key surface without a lot of effort. In fact, it's a case of "as played, so bought". If the leverage of the action feels comfortable and you have the feeling that you can nuance dynamically well, you are already far ahead. All the finer adjustment work is done afterwards anyway.

Now you have to narrow it down to the instruments you want. You can limit yourself to one manufacturer. You can limit yourself to one model. You are not forced to buy at this specific dealer. Once you've decided on a specific model, the dealer can also make an appointment with the manufacturer and you can select your personal instrument on the spot. This usually works out well, but if a premium dealer has picked out the fillet pieces shortly beforehand, the situation drastically changes. Then there are only a few weaker instruments to choose from and the selection manager looks embarrassed. He hopes for your ignorance and brand awareness. Fiddlesticks. In that case, a further search makes sense.

If you are not fixated on one brand, it is actually worth going to a dealer who carries several major brands. You can be sure that a serious dealer will not put any cucumbers in the store, which will then sooner or later become slow sellers. Actually, he takes the work out of pre-selecting them for you. Now it is your turn. Are you already clear about the size? Short or small instruments are forced to have thicker bass strings and therefore bring higher inharmonicities. Remember? It's unwanted, interfering harmonics, such as the ninth, seventh and fourth, which fight with each other, making chords or double stops in the lower bass range seem undefined. In clear words: it's acoustic garbage. Just sayin'.

Take a nose: Then open the instrument and take a nose —you sniff. If the instrument comes from Far Eastern production and smells a bit chemical, it's probably not what you want to have in your living room on the long haul.

Length counts: Upright—top lid open. Grand piano— open the lid and take music rack out. The melody section is always the problematic area with any piano. The note length is crucial here. Just play forte (don't bang, this distorts the result because the hammer head oscillates) and listen how long the note sounds. Five seconds are still okay; eight would be cool; three seconds are useless. For this, you'll have look on your wristwatch. If the eight-second tone swells a little bit in between before it says good-bye—we call this "trailing off"—this is quite desirable and musically helpful. But if the tone collapses after three seconds and then just continues to purr, it's no good. Normally, the octave between c" and c'" is relevant. It can always happen that there is an outlier between all the good notes. Then the technician is needed, because he can probably straighten it out—at least sometimes.

At high "altitudes": The last five notes of the instrument are telling. You open the pedal and strike one of the

last five notes. Take the a""—strike fortissimo and staccato and then listen into the instrument. If it makes a loud
"thump" and the loud attack noise immediately overruns
the note, that's unsatisfying. If you can clearly hear the
note flitting back and forth on the soundboard before it
disappears in the cloud of noise, you know that the
soundboard is active in high treble.

On the bridge: Now play a major triad in the middle
section in the root position. After one or two seconds,
open the pedal and listen to what happens. If the volume
increases audibly, the bridge distributes the energy of the
sides on the soundboard and thus does its job. If nothing
happens, the bridge is sluggish and your pedal work does
not conjure up any colorful interactions on the soundboard. Test different positions of the triad in the middle
position. Good luck.

Panorama on a grand piano: This is about the
acoustic and thus spatial imaging on the soundboard. If
the following triads come audibly from the hammer line,
then you know that the imaging in the room will not be
particularly three-dimensional and vivid. We are talking
about angle of incidence equals angle of reflection for the
stereophonic sound image. You now play major triads in
root position, following in thirds, over the whole middle
range, up and down, and listen to their positioning on the
soundboard. It also helps to trace the directions with

hand and arm in pointing mode—funnily enough, the arm and hand movement aids spatial hearing. If the panoramic image is clearly audible, the instrument will appear very vivid in space. Angle of incidence equals angle of reflection. If all triads come out flat from the hammer line, the spatial representation will be poor.

Attention transition: The transition to the bass section is critical for every instrument. The smaller the instrument, the more critical. For B, C and D grand pianos, the transition is at note 20, i.e. E/F. With smaller to very small instruments, this range can shift upwards by up to eleven notes. Even luxury instruments have problems with this. The nasal "ong" and "ang", which are particularly noticeable on smaller instruments, can be compensated for by a skilled piano tech. Since this is applied physics, this phenomenon will never completely disappear. By all means think onomatopoetically and listen for "ong" and "ang" to the left and right of the transition and its surroundings. If it is bearable, go ahead. It is not beautiful.

The Sostenuto: The right moment to focus on the sostenuto pedal, if the instrument of your choice offers this extravagant pedal. You open the right pedal, then step on the sostenuto pedal in the middle, then release the right pedal and watch the dampers drop in as you s l o w l y release the sostenuto pedal. Wait—were all the dampers up or were some not even considered? So, do the whole thing again. You release the middle pedal slowly. Do the dampers drop in reasonably evenly or does it pop left/right/front/back all over the place in a completely irregular manner? If it's completely chaotic and maybe some areas of the damping aren't even considered, then the technician will have to adjust a bit more.-100% accuracy cannot be achieved here. Nevertheless, we are grateful to have the part.

Damper bouncing on the grand piano: Press a black key silently whose damper now goes up. You hold it carefully and gently pull the damper up, checking for a little headroom until it noticeably docks against the damper rail. Up to 2 mm is still within the tolerance, from 3 mm you notice the recoil, respectively the fallback of the damper on the end of the key, i.e. under your finger. If it has no clearance at all, things are going in the wrong direction. The damper lifting spoon or damper lever then presses into the felt of the damper rail and the play appears rubbery—although it is not at all. In both cases, the technician has to recalibrate that. It's fiddly, but it's not rocket science. The technician will curse, though.

Now music may come: No, you don't have to "blow-dry" the salesperson now. An idea for the melody section: John Field—Nocturne in B flat major. Actually a bit unfair. Pretty bold arpeggios in the accompaniment work under the lone notes in the treble. This is clearly fortepi-ano literature. Here every modern instrument shows what it can do—or not. Can the left hand be finely gradu-ated and reduced? Does the melodic section carry long enough or do you have to sing along with the notes at the end? The second variation from Mozart's "Ah—vous di-rai-je, Maman" provides insight into the left hand's non-legato definition and, again, the carrying capacity of the melody. Gershwin's repetition stretta from "Rhapsody in Blue" puts the repetition components on fire. By now at the latest, you should have selected three favorites and can find your way to a secure result with further reper-toire of your choice.

What about a piano in my vacation home?

Enjoy Weekend and sunshine! In the vacation home, an instrument stands lonely and alone for a long time, only to be operated once a year. Maybe it stands by a lake or the sea. It can be cold and damp. The fresh sea air is poi-son for all center pins. Small flying creatures, i.e. moths, may also feed there on tasty hammers. Not a good place for a concert instrument. When I've gotten instruments for friends for such purposes, I've always gone for older, used, lightly played instruments. Why? The materials have left behind all tension conflicts due to age. Because they have a bit of clearence everywhere, they are less prone to jamming in damp conditions and don't take too badly to extreme temperatures and salty sea air. Should damage still occur, it's not a total disaster.

Thank you for calling the Piano Police. Always happy to help... I'll make a note in your file.
Over and out.

Bonus: On the Four Basic Parameters of Every Note

Greetings, I am here in the Practicing Patrol Car and conducting a boring observation on a popular pianist. Who? No names. But this is a good occasion to talk about articulation. First we got to cover the four basic parameters of every note for a better understanding.

No. 1 The Pitch. Very easy but essential: You just decide which note to play.

No. 2 The Velocity. It is about the speed with which the hammer head hits the string, also described as attack. This is decisive for the volume. All former shadings result from the secondary parameters such as key bed noise, post attack development, decay, etc.

No. 3 is the "note on" command, the moment when you press a key and the sound begins.

No. 4 is the "note off" command. This is the moment when you release the key and get damper closure. Caution: There's also the option of an incremental key release for a not audible damper closure and no fallback noise of the key. "Note on" and "note off" define the length of a note. The point where you put the "note off" is crucial for the articulation. Connecting to the next note, a "note off" at 100% length or more creates a legato. Longer than 100%: You achieve a super legato. Keep all overlaps the same length.

Note: All endings of slurs are soft. 50-75 % length creates a non legato. Below 50 % you are heading into the staccato zone. Normally: "No slur" is equivalent to non legato. A slur requires a legato. Play staccatos in designated areas only. And monitor the character of the piece. You dig that? Hope you do. Yes, always happy to help.

Pianist - Composer - Educator - Writer
Composer of the Fantastic Realism

I, Ratko Delorko, discovered the piano as my favourite toy at the tender age of three. It took me another three years to discover the piano as a creative tool for writing my youthful compositions.

My professional background—my formative years—were shaped by studying piano, composition and conducting in Cologne, Düsseldorf and Munich.

I have had the privilege of performing in such varied venues as the *Berlin Philharmonie*, the *Tonhalle* in Düsseldorf, the *Cologne Philharmonie*, the *Gasteig* in Munich, the *Philharmonie* in Essen, Hamburg's *Musikhalle*, the *Glocke* in Bremen, London's St. Martin in the Fields, *Paleau de la Musica* in Valencia, Beijing's Concert Hall, Shanghai's Oriental Arts Center, Cairo Opera House, St Paul's in Melbourne and others. Means: nearly 50 years of experience as a performing and recording artist are under my belt.

In my beloved program, entitled "The History of the Piano," I play compositions on 22 authentic instruments from different periods and narrate the development of the piano from its inception until the present day. To a

lesser degree, my musical inclinations also include performing jazz and rock music.

Music for solo piano, piano duet, chamber music, electronic music, opera and ballet are fields in which my
primary efforts are concentrated as a composer.

Currently, I lecture at the Frankfurt University of Music,
and I am a former lecturer at the Mozarteum in Salzburg
(2019-2021). In the past, I have conducted master class-
es and served as
guest professor in
Malaysia, Russia,
Italy, Croatia, the
US, Vietnam and
China, and I con-
tinue to do so to
the present day.

My book on the piano has been published by "Staccato-
Verlag, Düsseldorf". Recently my book, "The Nuts and
Bolts of Online Piano Teaching" has been released by
"Zeitklang - Music Production & Publishing." New: Ratko
Delorko's Piano Police Vol.I

https://www.delorko.com

Selected Productions:

 As the night falls: No, Chopin did not invent the Nocturne. It was the Irish composer John Field who captured nightly impressions musically.

https://listen.music-hub.com/Liqdev

 A pleasant Ragtime from the early 1900s. The composer, Robert Hampton, is not as famous as Scott Joplin, but truly a high quality composer of syncopated music.

https://listen.music-hub.com/BM8LR1

 Ratko Delorko performs on an original 1850 Klems (Düsseldorf) fortepiano.

https://listen.music-hub.com/EmhcLr

A cheeky and friendly sonata for fortepiano in two movements and with a smiling sideways glance at the galant style.

https://listen.music-hub.com/lKVhjM

A "Bagatelle" is, literally, something of little or no importance—a trifle. You don't need it, but it's nice to have.

https://listen.music-hub.com/sBXbFO

Fantasy is a form of condensed and composed improvisation. The repetitions are modified by ornamentation.

https://listen.music-hub.com/LcEOqy

The juvenile and rather stormy sonata in three movements was written in 1796-98, supported and sponsored by Anna Margarete von Browne, the wife of a Russian diplomat in Vienna.

https://listen.music-hub.com/yta1lE

A pounding prelude for a brisk fugue with a high chromatic content.

https://listen.music-hub.com/kI30X3

This sonata comes along like a little opera. A lovely aria here and a mighty tutti there, pumped with some recitativo secco.

https://listen.music-hub.com/L4O7Q7

My preferred Preludes and Fugues from the Well-Tempered Clavier Vol. II

https://listen.music-hub.com/soUCAX

I use an Upright GOLDON Toy Piano from the former GDR. Wooden hammers strike small steel rods in the matching frequency for sound generation.

https://listen.music-hub.com/RZKfPT

Twelve selected etudes from op. 10 and op. 25, live from the Berlin Philharmonic Hall

https://listen.music-hub.com/DnVJxC

One of the most popular Ragtimes by Scott Joplin, authentically recorded on an American Upright from the 1890s.

https://listen.music-hub.com/OnUhPr

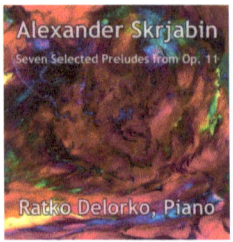

The 24 Preludes Op. 11 are a set of preludes based on Chopin's structure of defining the keys in his Preludes.

https://listen.music-hub.com/wuoDnS

A vast selection of encores from about 50 years on stage. The art of putting the keys on fire...

https://listen.music-hub.com/ImBBtE

My favorite pieces by Chick Corea, arranged in trilogy. Always suitable for a classical recital, too.

https://listen.music-hub.com/vZvMvO

My favorite Nocturnes by Frederic Chopin. Live from the Berlin Philharmonic Hall.

https://listen.music-hub.com/K8IIVS

For Ladislaus Dussek, the London piano maker John Broadwood extended the range of his instruments to 6 octaves. It is likely that he was the first to point the piano sideways to the audience, supposedly to be able to "present his shapely profile to the ladies".

https://listen.music-hub.com/FDQeY0

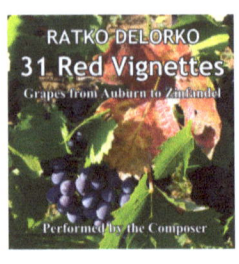

Red Grapes for Piano from Auburn to Zinfandel. In the past, the labels were placed on the neck of the bottle and documented the grape. The 31 short miniatures are condensed to the max. As always: Complexity in Simplicity.

https://listen.music-hub.com/IKJLkt

The "Pictures at an Exhibition" are based on pictures by the artist, Viktor Hartmann. A live recording from Essen's Philharmonic Hall. Cover art by Roberto Delorko (10 years old).

https://listen.music-hub.com/oG0rWx

The 12 tattoos represent a compact selection of classic tattoo designs. The representation always remains fantastic and tells of the stories that could be behind the illustration. And an attitude that you wear on your skin.

https://listen.music-hub.com/Ajnxbo

Quoting Mr. Prokofiev: "It will remain...in one movement: pretty, interesting, and practical." In a few words he describes one of the most technically demanding pieces he ever wrote for the piano.

https://listen.music-hub.com/5DSSug

The MIDI_Sonata for Piano and Synthetic Sounds is a kind of a modern time piano concerto. While there is an acoustic grand piano in the solo part, the accompanying synthetic sounds are trigged by a computer. The selected sounds are willingly artificial.

https://listen.music-hub.com/wxFM8h

The most beautiful variations by Wolfgang Amadeus Mozart: "Ah-Vous Dirai-je, Maman!" aka "Twinkle, Twinkle Little Star." A live recording by Ratko Delorko from the *Alte Oper* in Frankfurt.

https://listen.music-hub.com/XkK2zQ

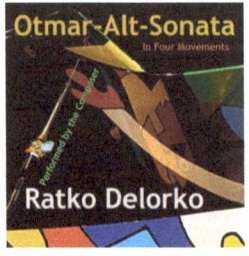

The conception of the Otmar-Alt-Sonata was developed in 1999 during a working stay at the Otmar Alt Foundation in Hamm - enveloped by the painter's works.

https://listen.music-hub.com/XkK2zQ

Rhapsody in Blue: The version of the Rhapsody in Blue for one piano commonly used today is necessarily heavily reduced. Ratko Delorko has created a new version for one pianist from the original two-piano version.

https://listen.music-hub.com/jJ2bT9

The piano cycle "Zeitklang" returns to the roots of the pianist composing in personal union for his own hand, who also plays the music in his own concerts. Only for his own hands? But no, for many other hands as well.

https://listen.music-hub.com/RS73kH

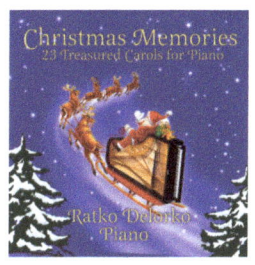

23 Treasured Christmas Carols for Piano: The idea of creating this Christmas recording was delivered from the feeling that I struggled to get a selection of great Christmas Carols at the piano that meet a standard I expect from every classical recording.

https://listen.music-hub.com/yFUonD

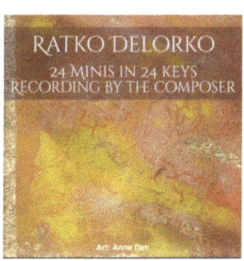

Let me take you on a pleasant journey through all 24 keys! The "24 Minis in all Keys for Piano" are short and very condensed piano pieces, which are also suitable for the fortepiano.

https://listen.music-hub.com/ELMDsM

The darkish piece "Dark Moon" was originally written for guitar. The colored flageolets can also be performed on the piano. So it made sense for me to arrange the work for the piano.

https://listen.music-hub.com/7umfy3

One of the most popular and beautiful piano pieces of impressionism.

https://listen.music-hub.com/hHeCLA

Beautiful romantic approach on a downstroke Fortepiano Stöcker from 1863. The highly romantic piano sounds like perfume.

https://listen.music-hub.com/Wvo7Su

A tiny and pensive Mazurka from my youthful days.

https://listen.music-hub.com/dlh1rA

Notes

Zeitfracht Medien GmbH
Ferdinand-Jühlke-Straße 7
99095 Erfurt, Deutschland
produktsicherheit@kolibri360.de